UKE **LIKE** THE PROS.com

# UKULELE
## BEGINNING MUSIC READING

*BY TERRY CARTER*

ISBN # 978-0-9826151-5-7

Copyright 2018

UKELIKETHEPROS.COM

# TABLE OF CONTENTS:

**UKE LIKE** THE PROS

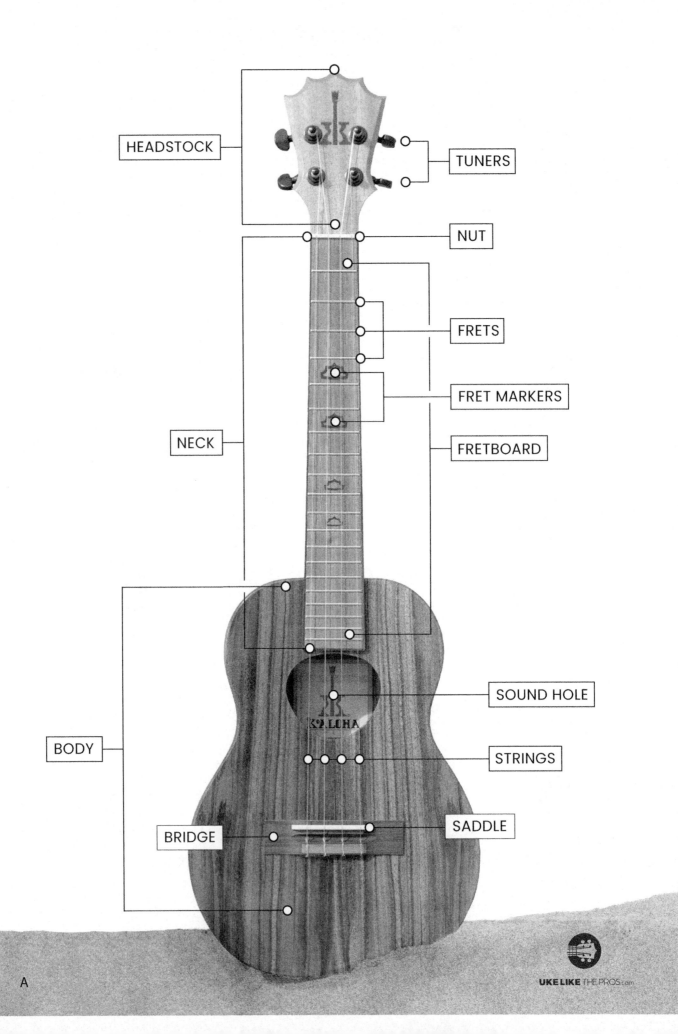

HEADSTOCK

TUNERS

NUT

FRETS

FRET MARKERS

FRETBOARD

NECK

SOUND HOLE

BODY

STRINGS

BRIDGE

SADDLE

A

# THE ESSENTIALS

It is important to learn and memorize these terms and symbols because they not only apply to Ukulele but to all music.

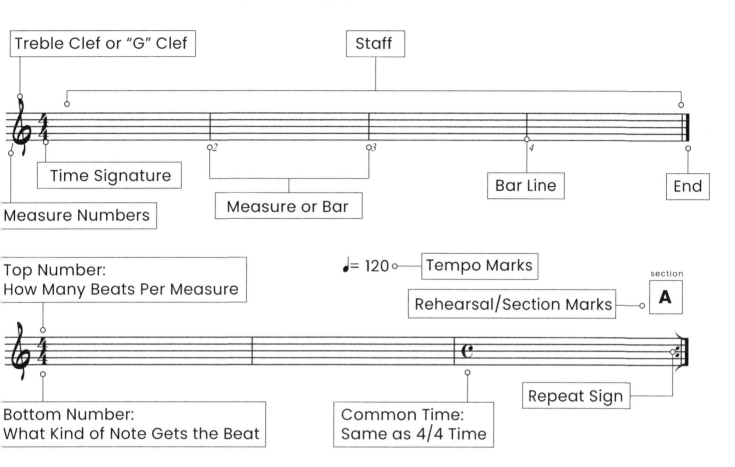

Treble Clef or "G" Clef

Staff

Time Signature

Measure Numbers

Measure or Bar

Bar Line

End

Top Number:
How Many Beats Per Measure

= 120 — Tempo Marks

section
A

Rehearsal/Section Marks

Bottom Number:
What Kind of Note Gets the Beat

Common Time:
Same as 4/4 Time

Repeat Sign

**Notes On The Staff:** There are seven notes in music (A, B, C, D, E, F, G) and they move up and down alphabetically on the staff.

G   A   B   C   D   E   F   G   A   B   C   D   E   F   G   A   B   C   D   E   F

**How To Remember The Notes:**

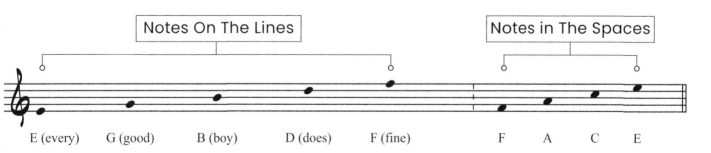

Notes On The Lines

Notes in The Spaces

E (every)   G (good)   B (boy)   D (does)   F (fine)        F   A   C   E

# MUSIC READING INTRODUCTION

Welcome to music reading on the ukulele. Whether you a total beginner to music reading or you have been doing it a while, this will be a great introduction to how to read music on the ukulele.

**Open String Notes (Ukulele's with High G String):**

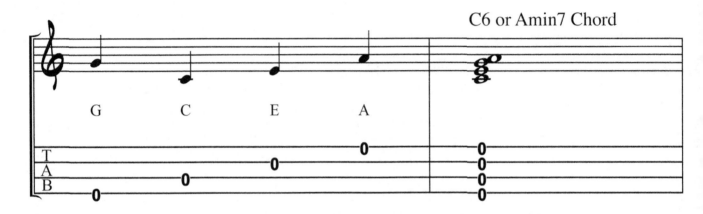

**Open String Notes (Ukulele's with Low G String)**

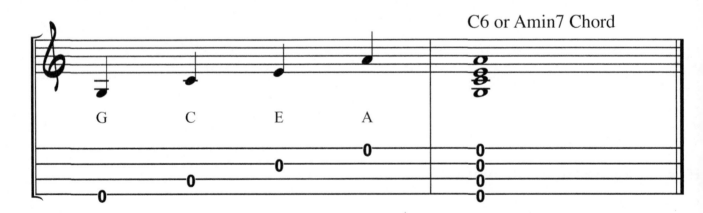

# NOTES ON THE UKULELE NECK

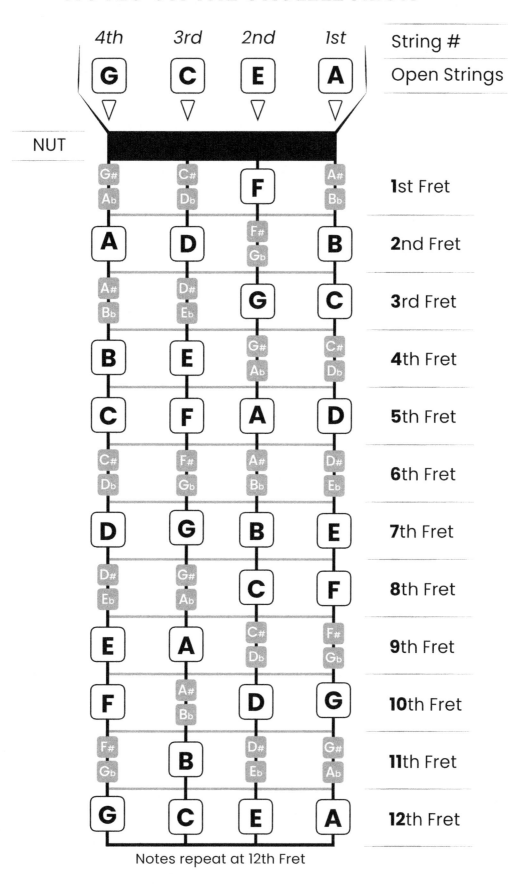

Notes repeat at 12th Fret

UKE LIKE THE PROS.com

D

# MUSIC SYMBOLS TO KNOW

A variety of symbols, articulations, repeats, hammer on's, pull off's, bends, and slides.

**Fermata:**
Hold note

**Staccato:**
Play note short

**Accent:**
Play note loud

**Accented Staccato:**
Play note
loud + short

**Vibrato**
Rapid "shaking"
of note

**Arpeggiated Chord:**
Play the notes in fast
succession from low
to high strings

**Grace Note:**
Fast embellishment
note played before
the main note

**Mute:**
"Muffle" sound of
strings either with
left or right hand

**Down Stroke:**
Pick string(s) with a
downward motion

**Up Stroke:**
Pick string(s) wi
an upward mot

**Tie:**
Play first note but
do not play second
note that it is tied to

**Ledger Lines:**
Extend the staff
higher or lower.

**Slash Notation:**
Repeat notes & rhythms
from previous measure

**1 Bar Repeat:**
Repeat notes &
rhythms from
previous measure

**2 Bar Repeat:**
Repeat notes & rhythms
from previous 2 measure

| **Repeat Sign:**<br>(Beginning) | **Repeat Sign:**<br>(End) |
|---|---|

| **1st Ending:**<br>Play this part the<br>first time only | **2nd Ending:**<br>Play this part<br>the second time |
|---|---|

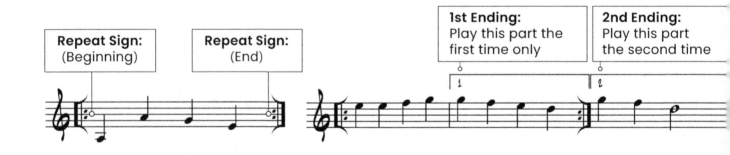

**(D.C. AL FINE)** — *D.C.* (da capo) means go to the beginning of the tune and stop when you get to FINE

**(D.C. AL CODA)** — *D.C.* means go to the beginning of the tune and jump to *Coda* 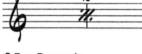 when you see the sign ⊕

**(D.S. AL FINE)** — *D.S.* (dal segno) means go to the *Sign* 𝄋 and stop when you get to FINE

**(D.S. AL CODA)** — *D.S.* means go to the *Sign* 𝄋 And Jump to the *Coda* ⊕ when you see ⊕

*SIM...* — Play the same rhythm, strum pattern, or picking pattern as the previous measure

*ETC...* — Continue the same rhythm, strum pattern, or picking pattern as the previous measure

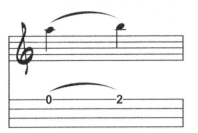

**Hammer On:**
Pick first note then hammer on
to the next note without picking it.

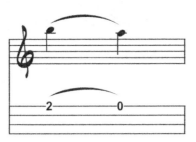

**Pull Off:**
Pick first note then pull off to
the next note without picking it.

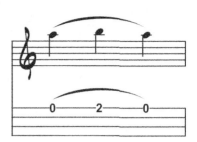

**Hammer On & Pull Off:**
Pick first note, hammer on to the
next note, and pull off to the last
note all in one motion.

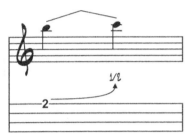

**1/2 Step Bend:**
Bend the first note
a 1/2 step or 1 fret.

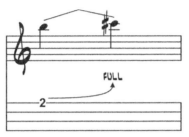

**Whole Step Bend:**
Bend the first note a whole
step or 2 frets.

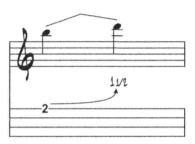

**Step & 1/2 Bend:**
Bend the first note
1 1/2 steps or 3 frets

**Forward Slide:**
Pick first note and slide
up to higher note.

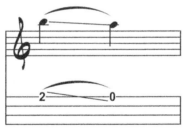

**Backward Slide:**
Pick first note and
slide back to lower note.

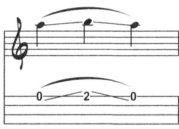

**Forward/Backward Slide:**
Pick first note, slide up to
next note and then slide back.

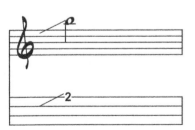

**Slide Into Note:**
Slide from 2-3 frets below note

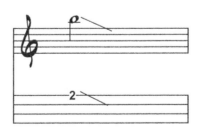

**Slide Off Note:**
Slide off 2-5 frets after note

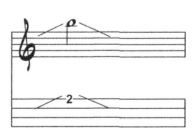

**Slide Into Note
then Slide Off Note**

# HOW TO FOLLOW ALONG ONLINE

If you are follwing the video course online at ukelikethepros.com each corresponding excercise is marked by the play icon ▶

If you see this icon (▶) it simply indicates the next excercise but that it is in the same video.

An example of this is below:

> All 3 of these examples are in the same video

▶ **Ex. 4 – 1** This exercise uses the **C & D notes** and is played using **whole notes.**

The note names have been written under each note to help you learn and identify the notes.

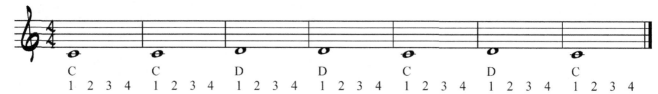

▶ **Ex. 4 – 2** This excercise still only uses the **C & D notes**, which are played using **half notes.**

▶ **Ex. 4 – 3** This excercise still uses the **C & D notes**, using **quarter notes.**

"If I miss a day of practice, I know it.
If I miss two days, my manager knows it.
If I miss three days, my audience knows it."


*- Andre Previn -*

# 01.

**CHAPTER**

# MUSIC READING
## 1st string

▶ Ex. 1 -1 and 1-2

▶ Ex. 1-3 and 1-4

▶ Ex. 1-5 and 1-6

▶ Ex. 1-7 "Fox Fire"

▶ Ex. 1-8 "Rush Hour"

▶ Ex. 1-9 "Coppola"

▶ Ex. 1-10 "The Trident"

We begin our first lesson in music reading in the open position by learning the **A, B, and C notes** on the "A" or the **first string.**

The "**A**" note is played by playing the **first string** with **no finger** on it.

The "**B**" note is located on the **second fret** of the **first string** and played with the **second finger.**

The "**C**" note is located on the **third fret** of the **first string** and is played with the **third finger.**

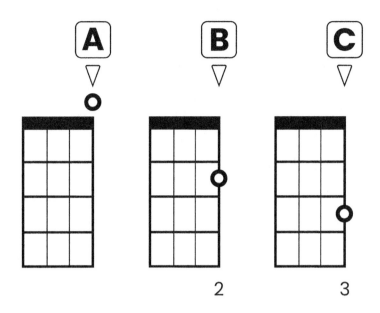

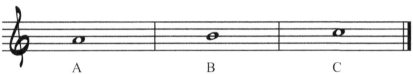

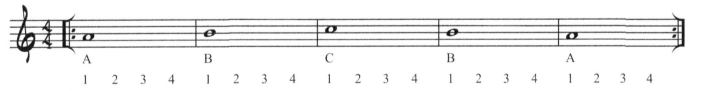

Ex. 1 - 1 This exercise uses the **A, B, & C notes** and is played using **whole notes.**
The note names have been written under each note to help you learn and identify the notes.

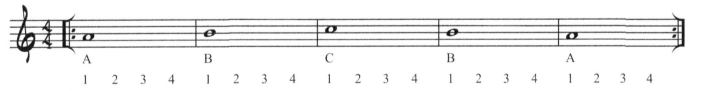

► Ex. 1 - 2
The **A, B, & C notes** are mixed up in this excercise but still only use **whole notes.**

### ▶ Ex. 1 - 3

This exercise **mainly** uses **half notes**. Notice the **repeat signs**.

### ▶ Ex. 1 - 4

This exercise uses **half notes**.

### ▶ Ex. 1 - 5

This exercise uses **quarter notes** and **half notes**.

### ▶ Ex. 1 - 6

This exercise uses **quarter notes** and **half notes**.

### ▶ Ex. 1 - 7 | "Fox Fire" *by Terry Carter*

This song will challenge your **dexterity** and **finger control**.

## Ex. 1 - 8 | "Rush Hour" *by Terry Carter*

Don't **rush** the tempo when switching from the **quarter notes** to the **eighth notes**.

## Ex. 1 - 9 | "Coppola" *by Terry Carter*

Are you talking to me?

## Ex. 1 - 10 | "The Trident" *by Terry Carter*

Notice that the **time signature** is **3/4** so **each measure** will have **3 beats**.

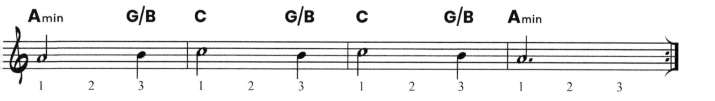

# 02.

**CHAPTER**

# MUSIC READING
## 2nd string

▶ Ex. 2-1, 2-2, and 2-3

▶ Ex. 2-4 Strings 1 + 2 Review

▶ Ex. 2-5 "Jump Street Blues"

▶ Ex. 2-6 "Twisted"

▶ Ex. 2-7 "King's Guard"

▶ Ex. 2-8 "Man of War"

Our second lesson in music reading in the open position introduces the **E, F, and G notes on the "E" or second string.**

The **"E" note** is played by playing the **second string** with **no finger** on it.

The **"F" note** is located on the **first fret** of the **second string** and played with the **first finger.**

The **"G" note** is located on the **third fret** of the **second string** and is played with the **third finger.**

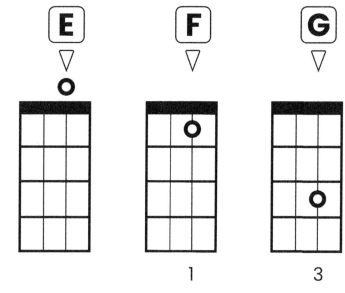

**Ex. 2 - 1** This exercise uses the **E, F, & G notes** and is played using **whole notes.**
The note names have been written under each note to help you learn and identify the notes.

**Ex. 2 - 2** This excercise still only uses the **E, F, & G notes,** which are played using **half notes.**

**Ex. 2 - 3** This excercise still uses the **E, F, & G notes,** using **quarter notes.**

### ▶ Ex. 2 - 4a

Review of **strings 1 + 2** using **whole notes**.

### ▶ Ex. 2 - 4b

Review of **strings 1 + 2** using **half notes**.

### ▶ Ex. 2 - 4c

Review of **strings 1 + 2** using **quarter notes**.

### ▶ Ex. 2 - 5 | "Jump Street Blues" *by Terry Carter*

The melody and chords give this a "bluesy" sound.

### Ex. 2 - 6 | "Twisted" *by Terry Carter*
This **melody jumps** back and fourth **between** the **1st** and **2nd strings**.

### Ex. 2 - 7 | "King's Guard" *by Terry Carter*
Pay attention to the **rhythm** as it **changes in certain measures**.

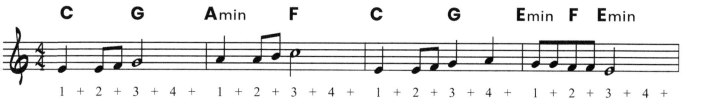

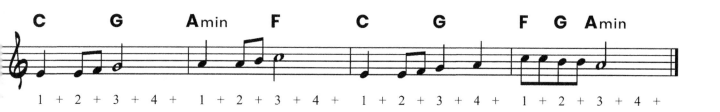

▶ **Ex. 2 - 8 |** "Man of War" *by Terry Carter*

This song is long and uses **all the notes we have learned** with **different rhythms.**

Notice the **time signature** is written in **COMMON TIME** (Same as **4/4**).

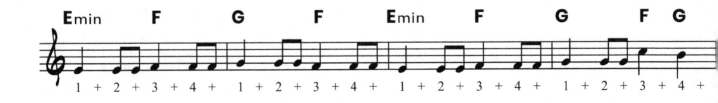

"You only get better by playing."

– *Buddy Rich* –

# 03.

**CHAPTER**

# MUSIC READING
## 1st + 2nd String Review

▶ Ex. 3-1 and 3-2

▶ Ex. 3-3 and 3-4

▶ Ex. 3-5 "Thor's Hammer"

**Ex. 3 - 1** First String using **Quarter Notes: A, B, & C**

**Ex. 3 - 2** First String using **Quarter & Eighth Notes: A, B, & C**

**Ex. 3 - 3** Second String using **Quarter Notes: E, F, & G**

**Ex. 3 - 4** Second String using **Quarter & Eighth Notes: E, F, & G**

**Ex. 3 - 5 | "Thor's Hammer"** *by Terry Carter* **(Strings 1 & 2)**

# 04.

**CHAPTER**

# MUSIC READING
## 3rd string

▶ Ex. 4-1, 4-2, and 4-3

▶ Ex. 4-4 Strings 1 - 3 Review

▶ Ex. 4-5 "Barn Burner"

▶ Ex. 4-6 "Big Iron"

▶ Ex. 4-7 "Blinky's Jig"

UKE LIKE THE PROS.com

This lesson in music reading introduces the C and D notes on the "C" or **third string**.

The "**C**" **note** is located on the **open third string**.

The "**D**" **note** is located on the **second fret** of the **third string** and is played with the **second finger**.

**TIP:** Memorize the placement of the C & D notes to make the reading easier when the notes on the 1st and 2nd strings are added to the exercises.

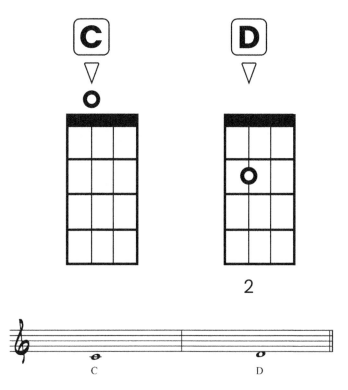

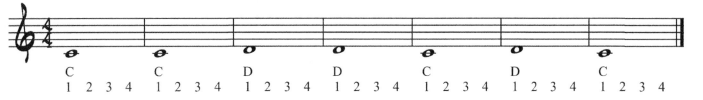

**Ex. 4 – 1** This exercise uses the **C & D notes** and is played using **whole notes**.
The note names have been written under each note to help you learn and identify the notes.

C       C       D       D       C       D       C
1 2 3 4   1 2 3 4   1 2 3 4   1 2 3 4   1 2 3 4   1 2 3 4   1 2 3 4

**Ex. 4 – 2** This excercise still only uses the **C & D notes**, which are played using **half notes**.

1   2   3   4   1   2   3   4   1   2   3   4   1   2   3   4

**Ex. 4 – 3** This excercise still uses the **C & D notes**, using **quarter notes**.

1   2   3   4   1   2   3   4   1   2   3   4   1   2   3   4

### Ex. 4 - 4 Review of strings 1-3 using whole notes

C  D  E  F  G  A  B  C  B  A  G  F  E  D  C

### Ex. 4 - 5 | "Barn Burner" *by Terry Carter*

This folk sounding song only works on the notes of the **2nd** and **3rd string.**

C      G      Amin      F      C      Amin      F      G

1 + 2 + 3 + 4 +   1 + 2 + 3 + 4 +   1 + 2 + 3 + 4 +   1 + 2 + 3 + 4 +

C      G      Amin      F      C      Amin      F  G  C

1 + 2 + 3 + 4 +   1 + 2 + 3 + 4 +   1 + 2 + 3 + 4 +   1 + 2 + 3 + 4 +

### Ex. 4 - 6 | "Big Iron" *by Terry Carter*

This rockin' song uses **repetition**, **5th chords** and **vibrato.**

D5   D5 F5   D5 C5 D5 G5   D5 C5 D5 F5   D5 C5 G5

1 + 2 + 3 + 4 +   1 + 2 + 3 + 4 +   1 + 2 + 3 + 4 +   1 + 2 + 3 + 4 +

D5 C5 D5 F5   D5 C5 D5 G5   D5 C5 D5 A5   G5 F5 D5

1 + 2 + 3 + 4 +   1 + 2 + 3 + 4 +   1 + 2 + 3 + 4 +   1 + 2 + 3 + 4 +

## Ex. 4 - 7 | "Blinky's Jig" *by Terry Carter*
This song sounds like a traditional Irish Jig, especially when played fast.

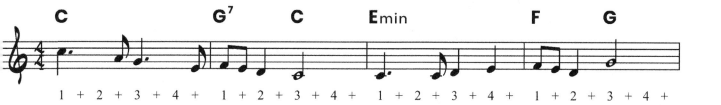

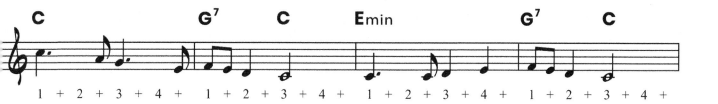

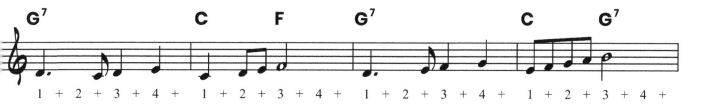

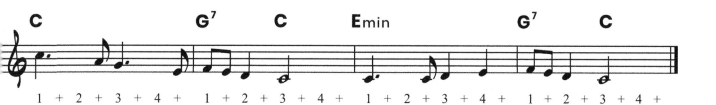

# 05.

# MUSIC READING
## Sharps (#) and Flats (b)

▶ Ex. 5-1 "Haunted March"

▶ Ex. 5-2 "Connecting the Dots"

▶ Ex. 5-3 "Yorkshire"

**Sharps (#)** are symbols that **raise a note up a 1/2 step (1 fret)** on the ukulele. That means the note will move **towards the "bridge"** of the ukulele **by "1" fret** and the **sound will get higher in pitch.** Play the examples below so you can hear how the sharps effect the sound of the notes.

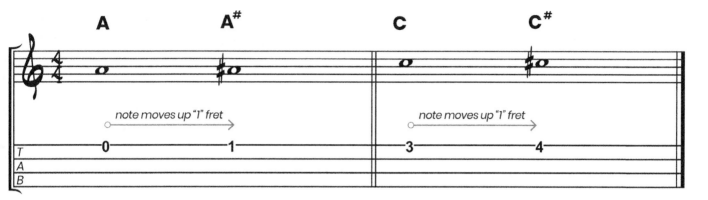

**Flats (♭)** are symbols that **lower a note down a 1/2 step (1 fret)** on the ukulele. That means the note will **move towards the "nut"** of the ukulele **by "1" fret** and the **sound will get lower in pitch.** Play the examples below so you can hear how the flats effect the sound of the notes.

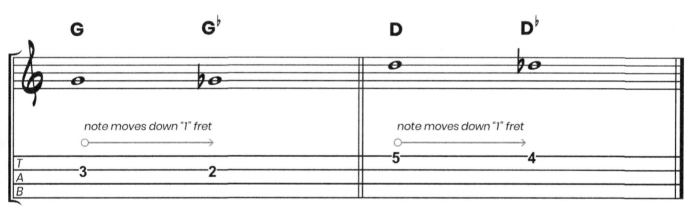

**SPECIAL RULES:** 1. You must **move UP to the next string** when you **FLAT a note that is an open string.**

2. **NATURAL SIGN ( ♮ ) cancels Sharps and Flats** and returns the note to it's original pitch.

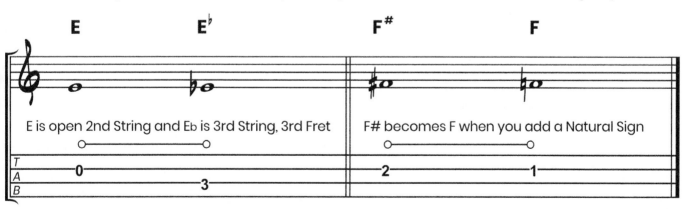

### ▶ Ex. 5 - 1 | "Haunted March" *by Terry Carter*

Notice the **low F# note** which is played on the **2nd fret** of the **low E string.**

There is also a **natural sign ( ♮ )** which **cancels** out **sharps ( # )** or **flats ( ♭ ).**

1 + 2 + 3 + 4 +   1 + 2 + 3 + 4 +   1 + 2 + 3 + 4 +   1 + 2 + 3 + 4 +

1 + 2 + 3 + 4 +   1 + 2 + 3 + 4 +   1 + 2 + 3 + 4 +   1 + 2 + 3 + 4 +

### ▶ Ex. 5 - 2 | "Connecting the Dots" *by Terry Carter*

**(Strings 1, 2, 3, and 4)**

### ▶ Ex. 5 - 3 | "Yorkshire" *by Terry Carter* **(Strings 1, 2, 3, and 4)**

"I am hitting my head against the walls,
but the walls are giving way."


- *Gustav Mahler* -

# 06.

**CHAPTER**

# MUSIC READING
## Strings 1-3 Review

▶ Ex. 6-1 Strings 1-3 Review

▶ Ex. 6-2 "Weeping Willow"

▶ Ex. 6-3 "Ode To Joy"

### Ex. 6 - 1a  Review of **strings 1-3** using **Whole Notes**

C    D    E    F    G    A    B    C    B    A    G    F    E    D    C

### Ex. 6 - 1b  Review of **strings 1-2** using **Half Notes**

1 2 3 4   1 2 3 4   1 2 3 4   1 2 3 4   1 2 3 4   1 2 3 4   1 2 3 4   1 2 3 4

### Ex. 6 - 1C  Review of **strings 1-2** using **Quarter Notes**

1    2    3    4    1    2    3    4    1    2    3    4    1    2    3    4

### Ex. 6 - 2  |  "Weeping Willow"  *by Terry Carter*

This one will test your finger dexterity using the "A" Minor Pentatonic.

1 + 2 + 3 + 4 +   1 + 2 + 3 + 4 +   1 + 2 + 3 + 4 +   1 + 2 + 3 + 4 +

1 + 2 + 3 + 4 +   1 + 2 + 3 + 4 +   1 + 2 + 3 + 4 +   1 + 2 + 3 + 4 +

### ▶ Ex. 6 - 3 | "Ode To Joy" *by Ludwig Van Beethoven*

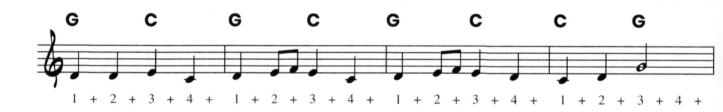

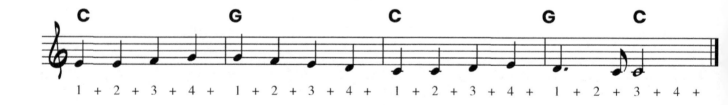

"Dream big, reach for the stars,
you are only held back by your thoughts"

*- Terry Carter -*

# 07.

**CHAPTER**

# MUSIC READING
## High Note Reading

▶ Ex. 7-1 "Amazing Grace"

▶ Ex. 7-2 "Groovin' The Blues"

▶ Ex. 7-3 "An After Thought"

▶ Ex. 7-4 "Waltz For Heather"

## Ex. 7 - 1 | "Amazing Grace" *by John Newton*

This song is in **3/4 time**. It **uses a pickup note** which means that the **first note** of the song starts on beat 3. This tune **also uses a TIE** that **connects two notes,** meaning that you **play the first note but don't play the second note** that it is tied to but continue to let the note ring out.

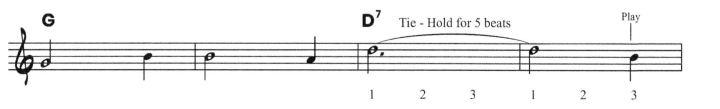

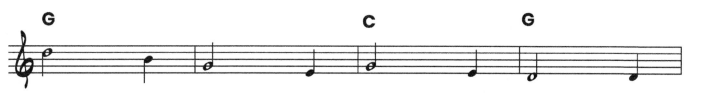

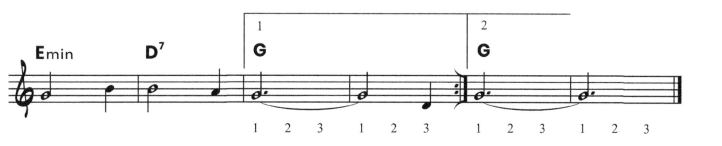

▶ ### Ex. 7 - 2 | "Groovin' The Blues" *by Terry Carter*

♩=84

Swing (shuffle) Feel.

This tune is based on the Blues Shuffle in "A." Although there are a lot of **eighth notes**, there are a lot of repeated patterns.

▶ ### Ex. 7 - 3 | "An After Thought" *by Terry Carter*

This song **goes up to the high F note** on the **1st string**.

## Ex. 7 - 4 | "Waltz for Heather" *by Terry Carter*

The **time signature** for this song is **3/4** and **uses a dotted half note** which gets **3 beats.** This song **goes up to the high F note.**

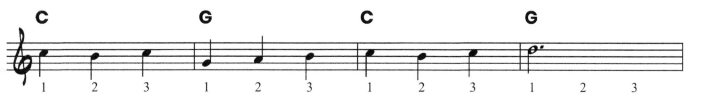

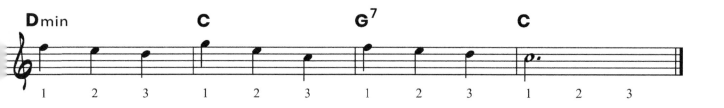

# 08.
CHAPTER

# MUSIC READING
# Americano Songs

## Ex. 8 - 1 | "Oh' Susana"

This song is in the key of D Major (F# and C#) and uses a pickup on beat 4.

## ▶ Ex. 8 - 2 | "Aura Lee"

An American Civil War song written by W.W. Fosdick and George R. Poulton.
Elvis Presley adapted this melody in his song, "Love Me Tender."

## Ex. 8 - 3 | "Yankee Doodle"

This is a simple and fun patriotic song to play. The lyrics were believed to be written by Dr. Shackburg around 1755.

## Ex. 8 - 4 | "Wildwood Flower"

This song is in the **key of D (F# and C#)**. It also **goes up to the high F#.**

# 09.

# MUSIC READING
## Low G String

▶ Ex. 9-1, 9-2, and 9-3

▶ Ex. 9-4 Strings 1-4 Review

▶ Ex. 9-5 "S'wish"

▶ Ex. 9-6 "Waiting For You"

▶ Ex. 9-7 "Cedarwood"

▶ Ex. 9-8 "Barking Crickets"

In this lesson we are looking at the "G", "A", and "B" notes on the Low "G" or 4th string.

The "G" note is played by playing the fourth string open.

The "A" note is located on the second fret of the fourth string and played with the second finger.

The "B" note is located on the fourth fret of the fourth string and is played with the fourth finger.

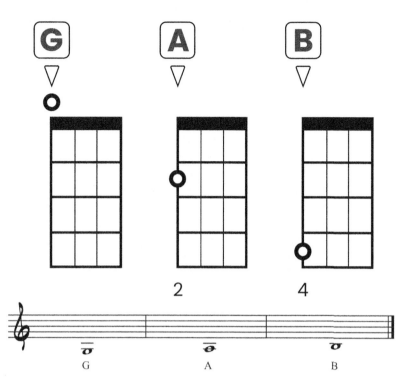

Ex. 9 - 1 This exercise uses the G, A, & B notes and is played using whole notes.
The note names have been written under each note to help you learn and identify the notes.

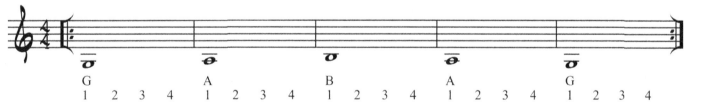

Ex. 9 - 2 This excercise still only uses the G, A, & B notes, which are played using half notes.

Ex. 9 - 3 This excercise still uses the G, A, & B notes, using quarter notes.

▶ **Ex. 9 - 4a** Review of **strings 1-4** using **Whole Notes**

G A B C D E F G A B C B A G F E D C B A G

▶ **Ex. 9 - 4b** Review of **strings 1-4** using **Half Notes**

▶ **Ex. 9 - 4c** Review of **strings 1-4** using **Quarter Notes**

▶ **Ex. 9 - 5 |** **"S'wish"** *by Terry Carter*
This song is going to focus on the **low 4 strings.**

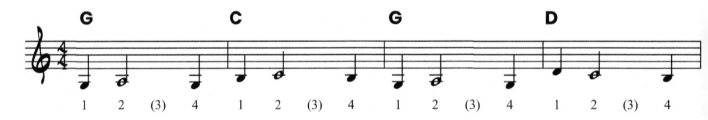

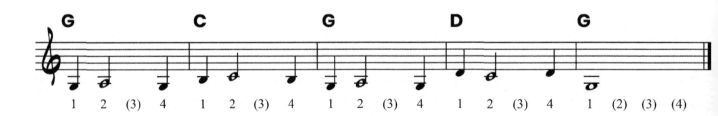

UKE LIKE THE PROS.com

## Ex. 9 – 6 | "Waiting For You" *by Terry Carter*

This song not only sounds great but gives you practice on the **Low G string**.

## Ex. 9 – 7 | "Cedarwood" *by Terry Carter*

This happy litle ditty will test your reading with **dotted quarter notes**.

## Ex. 9 – 8 | "Barking Crickets" *by Terry Carter*

These crickets don't give you a break until you finish the song.

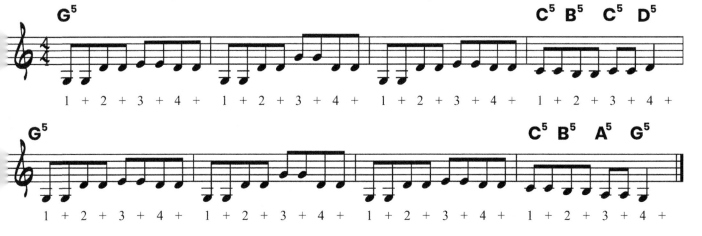

UKE LIKE THE PROS.com

# 10.

**CHAPTER**

# MUSIC READING
## Your Final Test

- ▶ Ex. 10-1 [DUET] "Outlaw's Revenge" Uke 1
- ▶ Ex. 10-2 [DUET] "Outlaw's Revenge" Uke 2 (High)
- ▶ Ex. 10-3 [DUET] "Outlaw's Revenge" Uke 2 (Low)
- ▶ Ex. 10-4 "Spitfire"

UKE LIKE THE PROS.com

# Ex. 10 - 1 | "Outlaw's Revenge" *by Terry Carter*
This **duet** uses **strings 1-3** and has **3 sections:** [ A ] - [ B ] - [ C ]

THIS VIDEO ▶ LESSON
WILL TEACH **UKE 1**

## Ex. 10 - 2 | "Outlaw's Revenge" *by Terry Carter*

This **duet** uses **strings 1-3** and has **3 sections:** [ A ] - [ B ] - [ C ]

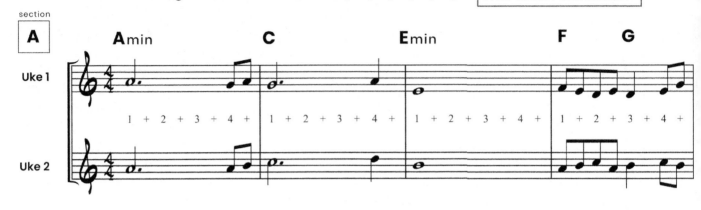

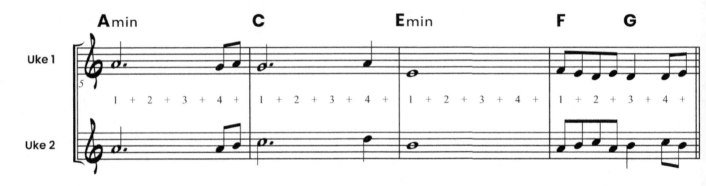

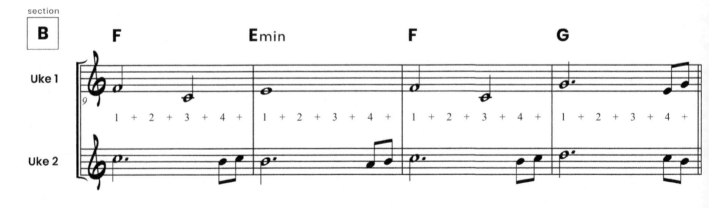

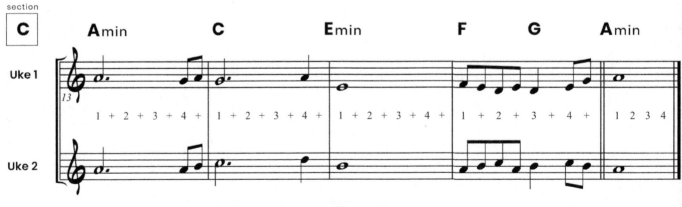

UKE LIKE THE PROS.com

## Ex. 10 - 3 | "Outlaw's Revenge" *by Terry Carter*
This **duet** uses **strings 1-3** and has **3 sections:** [ A ] - [ B ] - [ C ]

THIS VIDEO ▶ LESSON
WILL TEACH **UKE 2 LOW**

## Ex. 10 – 4 | "Spitfire" *by Terry Carter*

1 + 2 + 3 + 4 + 1 + 2 + 3 + 4 + 1 + 2 + 3 + 4 + 1 + 2 + 3 + 4 +

1 + 2 + 3 + 4 + 1 + 2 + 3 + 4 + 1 + 2 + 3 + 4 + 1 + 2 + 3 + 4 +

1 + 2 + 3 + 4 + 1 + 2 + 3 + 4 + 1 + 2 + 3 + 4 + 1 + 2 + 3 + 4 +

1 + 2 + 3 + 4 + 1 + 2 + 3 + 4 + 1 + 2 + 3 + 4 + 1 + 2 + 3 + 4 +

1 + 2 + 3 + 4 + 1 + 2 + 3 + 4 + 1 + 2 + 3 + 4 + 1 + 2 +

1 + 2 + 3 + 4 + 1 + 2 + 3 + 4 + 1 2 3 4

Printed in Great Britain
by Amazon

38855388R00031